THE SECR
of The
HUNGRY MONK

as extracted from Ian Dowding
by Nigel and Susan Mackenzie

HUNGRY MONK PUBLICATIONS
Jevington
Near Polegate
Sussex

Also in the same series
The Deeper Secrets of the Hungry Monk
The Hungry Monk at Home
The Secret Sauce Book of the Hungry Monk
Cooking with the Hungry Monk
The Hungry Monk at Work

First published December 1971
Second edition September 1972
Third edition November 1973
Fourth edition August 1974
Fifth edition April 1975
Sixth edition October 1976
Seventh edition July 1977
Eighth edition September 1979
Ninth edition January 1983
Tenth edition January 1985
Eleventh edition November 1991

INTRODUCTION

When we first opened The Hungry Monk we had a clear idea not only of the sort of dishes that we wanted to serve, but more precisely the 'personality' that the food should have. To this end we were incredibly lucky to have Ian Dowding as our first head chef — he immediately grasped exactly what was wanted.

The two elements that we considered crucial to this 'personality' were depth of flavour and texture. The food had to be tasty rather than rich, interesting to eat rather than beautiful to look at. Caulibiac of Salmon is a perfect example with its juicy interior of salmon and stuffed pancakes wrapped in a crisp case of puff pastry. The flavour is sealed in. The texture is full of variety.

After four years The Hungry Monk had developed and refined a number of such dishes for which people returned again and again. This book started life as a sort of kitchen manual to consolidate and perpetuate this repetoire.

Now in it's seventh edition and rating to our amazement among the best selling paper-back cookbooks in the country — it has proved itself to have a wide appeal to novice and experienced cook alike.

Since 1971 when this book was first published, many new ideas have been hatched. In 1974 we published a sequel — "The Deeper Secrets of The Hungry Monk" as a companion volume. In both cases we are indebted to Graham Jeffrey for peppering the pages with his charming drawings of monastery life.

N. A. M.
JUNE, 1977

CONTENTS

Beef *continued*

THE HUNGRY MONK'S BROWN BREAD ROLLS

To make 16 rolls

2 pounds wholemeal flour
3 ounces butter
1 dessertspoon salt
½ teaspoon sugar
½ ounce yeast
1 pint lukewarm water

Preparation
Sift the flour with the salt into a warmed bowl
Preheat the oven to number 8-475 degrees

Method
Firstly cream the yeast with the warm water and sugar and leave to ferment.
While this is happening rub the butter and flour together, finishing by
leaving a well in the centre. By the time you have completed this the yeast
and water should be frothy and ready to be poured into the well in the
middle of the flour. Work into a dough.

The time has come to start kneading and this is best done by placing the
lump of dough on the table and, taking the outer edge, pull it into the
middle of the dough and press it down with the heel of your hand.
Continue kneading the dough in this way while gradually revolving it. The
longer that you can face this strenuous exercise the better your bread will be.

Once this has been done, allow the dough to stand in a warm place until,
through the action of the yeast, it has doubled its bulk.

Finally knead the dough again for a few moments to expel the air before
proceeding to cut off two ounce chunks, rolling each one lightly into a ball.
Once again the dough will start expanding. Wait until it has increased in
size by half and then put into a hot oven (number 8-475 degrees) for 40
minutes until brown and crusty. These rolls, like all bread, are at their best
when served warm.

❀

Hints. If 16 rolls are too big a batch, put some in the deep freeze.

❀

Variation
To make white rolls there is no need to alter this recipe in any other way
than to use white flour.

COLD AVOCADO and LEMON SOUP

The most perfect starter for summer eating. A welcome variation on the hard worn theme of Avocado Pear.

To serve 6

3 ripe avocados
4 lemons
chopped parsley
1½ pints of good chicken or veal stock
½ pint single cream
salt and white pepper

Method
Peel and stone the avocados. Place in a mixing bowl, with the juice of three lemons. Beat to a smooth consistency, add the parsley, seasoning and stock. Stir for a few minutes before blending in the cream. Pour into a serving bowl and chill thoroughly. Just before serving, sprinkle a little parsley and decorate with sliced lemons.

Hints. Use only stainless steel, wood or china utensils to avoid tainting.

Variation
Add a dash of curry powder.

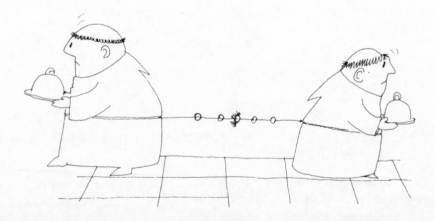

CRAB
and SWEETCORN SOUP

A warming start to a winter dinner party.

To serve 4

3 ounces butter
8 ounces fresh crab meat (or good frozen or tinned etc.)
a sprig of fennel
salt and black pepper
3 ounces flour
2 pints fish stock
4 ounces sweetcorn — tinned
¼ pint single cream
tabasco

Preparation
Flake the crab meat.

Method
Melt the butter in a pan with the crab meat, fennel and seasoning. Fry gently for a few moments before adding the flour. Stir constantly for five minutes until a smooth consistency has been achieved. Add the fish stock, bring to the boil and simmer for 15 minutes. Finally add the sweetcorn, two shakes of tabasco and the cream. Serve immediately

*"Nobody else grows fresh vegetables
like you do."*

CHILLED GREEN VEGETABLE SOUP

This is a particularly attractive soup and makes the most of the colour and crispness of summer vegetables.

To serve 6 — 8

1 pound potatoes
1½ pints milk
1 small clove of garlic
salt and white pepper
8 ounces cream cheese
½ pint dry white wine
½ pint single cream
1 ounce green of leek
1 ounce watercress including stalk
1 ounce mustard and cress } finely chopped
1 ounce parsley
1 ounce crisp lettuce hearts
2 ounces cucumber — unpeeled

Preparation
Peel and slice the potatoes, crush the garlic.

Method
Poach the potatoes in the milk with the garlic and seasoning until soft. Pass through a sieve together with the cream cheese. Stir. Add the white wine and cream and then chill. Only when you are ready to serve should the vegetables be added if they are to be as crisp and fresh as intended. Adjust the seasoning.

Variation
Do not be afraid to use vegetables other than those mentioned.

CHILLED TOMATO and ORANGE SOUP

This rivals Gazpacho for a clean tasting and refreshing starter.

To serve 6

2 pounds tomatoes
2 oranges
½ onion
¼ pint white wine
1 tablespoon vinegar
1 tablespoon oil
1½ pints chicken stock
2 ounces fresh white breadcrumbs
chopped parsley
salt and black pepper

Method

Peel the zest from the oranges taking care to remove any pith. Cut the zest into very thin strips for the best flavour and presentation. Remove the pith and fillet the orange into segments. Peel the tomatoes and onions and chop very finely. Combine the above ingredients with the oil, vinegar, wine and stock. Stir well and add all the remaining ingredients — season to taste and allow to stand in the refrigerator for at least 12 hours.

Just before serving, stir in the freshly chopped parsley and accompany with croutons if you wish.

SEAFOOD SOUP

A spicy and original way of bringing the full flavour out of seafood. This especially applies where frozen prawns are used.

To serve 6

2 pints fresh mussels
6 ounces prawns
1¾ pounds of white fish — halibut, sole or hake — filleted and skinned
8 ounces eel

2 tablespoons of olive oil
1 clove of garlic
½ Spanish onion
parsley
1 green chilli
salt and black pepper
½ pint dry white wine

8 ounces tomatoes
1 tablespoon of tomato puree
a sprig of fennel
1 bay leaf
juice of a lemon
a pinch of caraway seeds

Preparation
Wash the mussels and remove the beards. Take a large pan and pour enough of the wine to cover the bottom, 1 inch deep. Bring to the boil and add the mussels. Cover and boil until the mussels are open (about five minutes). This will yield good stock which should be drained off into a jug.

Chop the raw white fish and eel into small cubes. Peel, seed and roughly chop the tomatoes. Chop finely the onion, green chilli and parsley. Crush the garlic.

Method
Heat the oil in a large saucepan and add the chopped white fish, eel, garlic, onion, parsley, chilli and seasoning. Fry slowly, stirring all the time until the fish is cooked and beginning to flake. Make up the mussel stock to two pints with water and pour into the saucepan together with the remaining white wine. Bring to the boil and simmer adding all the remaining ingredients except for the mussels and prawns. Cook for 15 minutes, stirring occasionally. Lastly, just before serving, add the prawns and mussels.

Hints. The mussels may well leave a sediment in the cooling stock which on no account must find its way into the soup.

Variations
Serve with a dollop of sour cream. Just about any fish can be used.

STILTON and ONION SOUP

A very savoury country soup for cold days.

To serve 4

3 ounces butter
1 Spanish onion
6 ounces Stilton cheese
3 ounces flour
2 pints chicken stock
a bay leaf
salt and black pepper
¼ pint single cream

Preparation
Thinly slice the onion, crumble the Stilton.

Method
Melt the butter in a pan and add the sliced onion. Fry gently until soft and
then add the Stilton. Stir with a wooden spoon until the Stilton melts to
form a smooth cream. Add the flour and cook for a further five minutes,
stirring all the time before adding the chicken stock, bay leaf and seasoning.
Bring to the boil and simmer for 20 minutes. Remove the bay leaf. Finally,
add the cream and serve immediately.

FISH STARTERS

BOMBAY HERRINGS

This dish is equally suitable as a snack or a starter and certainly gives the much under-used herring a new lease of life.

To serve 6

6 herrings with soft roes
lemon zest
pepper corns
a bay leaf
a small onion
1 packet of thinly sliced rye bread
½ pint home made mayonnaise
1 heaped dessertspoon curry powder
1 small eating apple

Preparation
Fillet and skin the herrings and roll each fillet round a soft roe. Chop the apple and slice the onion. Preheat the oven to number 3-350 degrees.

Method
Place the rolled herrings tightly packed into a shallow fireproof dish. Pour over water and add the lemon zest, pepper corns, bay leaf and sliced onion. Cover and poach for 30 minutes in a low oven. Cool and drain.

Spread the rye bread with butter and arrange two rolls of herring on each piece. Mix the curry powder into the mayonnaise with the chopped apple and coat the fish generously. Garnish with lettuce hearts and orange slices.

BRANDADE de MORUE

A subtle flavoured fish pate made with cod and brought to life with garlic, black pepper and lemon juice.

To serve 4 — 6

1 pound fresh or salt cod — filleted
¼ pint oil
juice of 2 lemons
3 cloves of garlic
2 tablespoonfuls fresh white breadcrumbs
1 gill double cream
salt and black pepper

Preparation

If using salt cod, soak in plenty of cold water overnight to remove excess salt. Chop the cod roughly into cubes. Crush the garlic. Preheat the oven to number 5-400 degrees.

Method

Stew the cod in the oil until the fish goes mushy. Stir occasionally and as you do so, add the seasoning, garlic and lemon juice. If you are using salt cod do not add any more salt. In both cases use plenty of black pepper. Take the pan off the heat and add the cream and breadcrumbs and beat the mixture hard to a creamy consistency. Spoon into a fire-proof pate-dish or loaf tin and bake in a moderately hot oven (number 5-400 degrees) for approximately 45 minutes until a crisp and golden crust has formed.

Put in a cool place and allow to set.

Finally turn the Brandade out and garnish with pieces of lemon. Serve with freshly fried croutes.

CRAB QUICHE

A crisp open flan filled with a mixture of crab meat, eggs and cream,
lightly baked.

To serve 6

¾ pound crab meat frozen or fresh, using both the dark and light meat
1 large egg
1 gill of fresh or soured double cream
juice of ½ lemon
dash of tabasco
salt and black pepper
½ small onion
8 ounces short crust pastry

Preparation
Line an 8 inch flan case thinly with the pastry. Finely chop the onion.
Preheat the oven to number 6-425 degrees.

Method
Beat the egg into the cream before gently folding in all the other ingredients.
Season to taste and pour into the uncooked pastry case. Cook in a hot
oven (number 6-425 degrees) for 30 minutes or until you have a delicious
looking golden brown Quiche. Serve warm.

Hint. This is an excellent dish for the freezer.

Variation
Lobster meat and most other shellfish would do equally well in place of
crab meat.

CRISPY MUSSELS
in SWEET and SOUR SAUCE

These taste as good as they sound. Each mussel is taken out of its shell, cooked in a crisp covering of breadcrumbs and served on a bed of rice with sweet and sour sauce.

To serve 6

The Mussels
1 gallon of large mussels
seasoned flour
2 eggs
1 cup of milk
fresh white breadcrumbs
2 cupfuls of rice
water

Sweet and Sour Sauce
1 small tin pineapple chunks and their juice (chopped finely)
3 dessertspoons vinegar
1 tablespoon soy sauce
2 dessertspoons demerara sugar
a glass of dry sherry
1 large carrot — grated
1 green pepper (chopped finely)
½ onion (chopped finely)
1 clove of garlic
2 ounces butter
2 ounces flour

Preparation

Wash the mussels and remove beards. Steam to open the shells (see page 12 Seafood Soup) retaining the stock. Remove the mussels from the shells and put on a cloth to drain. Boil the rice in four cups of water with a large pinch of salt. Make up the egg wash by beating the eggs and milk together.

Method

Separate the ingredients into two groups as follows:—

The pineapple juice
Vinegar
Soy Sauce   Group 1
Demerara sugar
Sherry

Carrot
Green pepper
Onion } Group 2
Garlic
Pineapple

Place all the ingredients from Group 1 in a saucepan and make up to 1½ pints, by adding the stock from the mussels — stir thoroughly but do not cook. Set aside.

Take all the ingredients from Group 2 and fry them with the butter for four minutes over a gentle heat. Sprinkle in the flour and continue to cook stirring briskly. Add the Group 1 liquor, bring to the boil, cover and allow to bubble gently for 15-20 minutes.

While this is happening you have the opportunity to individually flour, egg and breadcrumb the mussels.

Your sweet and sour sauce should now be ready. Increase the sweetness or sourness with sugar or vinegar respectively, according to taste. Shortly before serving, the mussels should be deep fried until crisp in very hot fat. Finally place the mussels on a bed of the rice and serve the hot sweet and sour sauce separately.

HOT SUSSEX SMOKIE

Without any question the most popular starter at The Hungry Monk. Little pots filled with a mixture of smoked haddock flaked into a rich cheese sauce with a crisp Parmesan topping.

To serve 6

1 pound filleted and skinned smoked haddock
2 ounces butter
2 ounces flour
4 ounces cheddar cheese
1 glass of dry white wine
black pepper
1 bay leaf
grated Parmesan cheese

Preparation
Poach the haddock in 1½ pints of water with the bay leaf. Cool slightly. Grate the cheddar cheese.

Method
Melt the butter in a saucepan and add the flour to form a roux. After two or three minutes when the flour is fully cooked take one pint of the stock from the poached haddock and pour in slowly, stirring all the time. Bring to the boil and simmer for 15 minutes stirring occasionally. Add the cheddar cheese, black pepper and wine. Continue to cook until you have achieved a smooth cheese sauce. Finally flake in the haddock and spoon the mixture into six small ramekins. Sprinkle Parmesan on the top of each.

If you are serving immediately, flash under the grill until the Parmesan goes golden brown, otherwise bake in a hot oven for 10 minutes before serving.   ❦

Hint. It is perfectly possible to use smoked cod — indeed it has the advantage of being cheaper and less bony.

KIPPERS IN CREAM
and CURRY SAUCE

A variation on the theme of Hot Sussex Smokie.

To serve 4

1 pound kipper fillets
1 bay leaf
water
2 ounces butter
a dessertspoon curry powder
1 small eating apple
2 ounces flour
1 gill of double cream

Preparation
Poach the kipper fillets in 1½ pints of water with the bay leaf.

Method
Melt the butter in a saucepan. Grate the apple straight into the
butter and add the curry powder. Sprinkle in the flour to make a roux
and stir for two or three minutes until the flour is fully cooked. Slowly
pour in one pint of the stock from the poached kippers and bring to the
boil stirring briskly. Simmer for 15 minutes before removing from the heat.
Blend in the cream. Flake in the kippers and ladle into four ramekins.
Dollop a spoonful of cream on the top of each dish and flash under the
grill. Eat immediately. ⚜

Variation
For a delicious Sunday breakfast keep the kipper fillets whole and pour
the cream and curry sauce over them.

PRAWNS and ONIONS in CREAM CHEESE

A cream cheese based pate.

To serve 6

8 ounces prawns
½ onion
8 ounces cream cheese
juice of 1 lemon
black pepper

Preparation
Beat the cream cheese until it is soft and shining. Slice the onion.

Method
Fry the prawns and onions in butter until the onions turn golden. Fold into the cream cheese. Finally add lemon juice and black pepper. Chill. Serve on rye bread as an open sandwich or with hot french bread or toast.

FRESH SARDINES

To a nation raised on tinned sardines it is almost impossible to imagine how deliciously different a fresh sardine is. The problem is getting them. Myall and Sons of Romilly Street, Soho are one of the most dependable sources of supply and seem quite prepared to send a box by passenger train any reasonable distance from London. Telephone 01-437 4063.

Our favourite ways of cooking sardines
(There is no need to gut fresh sardines)

Provencale
Pass the sardines through seasoned flour and fry them for a few minutes on each side in butter with onions and garlic. Add white wine, chopped tomatoes and seasoning. Cover and simmer for five minutes. Sprinkle with chopped parsley.

Grilled sardines with herb and garlic butter
Pass through seasoned flour and brush with olive oil or butter and grill four minutes on each side. Meanwhile melt a small pot of butter together with crushed garlic and herbs. Cook until golden. Finally add a squeeze of lemon juice and while the butter is still frothing, pour it over the sardines.

Charcoal-grilled sardines
To many people sardines are at their best brushed with oil and cooked on an open charcoal grill by the sea, preferably accompanied by a large bottle of dry white wine.

TARAMOSALATA

A classic Greek smoked fish pate with a unique flavour. Light and savoury, it is an ideal appetizer for jaded palates.

Plenty for 8

6 ounces smoked cod's roe
12 slices white bread
2 cloves of garlic
¼ Spanish onion
juice of 2 lemons
black pepper
16 tablespoons oil

Preparation
Trim crusts off bread and soak in water. Grate the onions. Crush the garlic.

Method
Squeeze the bread dry and pound it together with the roe, onion, garlic, lemon juice and black pepper and continue to beat while gradually introducing the oil until the mixture becomes smooth and creamy. Sometimes it is necessary at this stage to add further oil or lemon juice according to taste. Serve with piping hot toast.

MEAT AND VEGETABLE STARTERS

FARMHOUSE TERRINE

Our own liver pate. This Terrine can serve anything between 8 to 12 people depending on their appetite.

8 ounces duck liver and/or chicken liver
8 ounces minced raw pork liver
8 ounces minced raw pork
4 ounces minced raw ham
1 pound streaky bacon
2 ounces butter
1 onion
3 cloves of garlic
1 large tot of brandy
1 wine glass of strong red wine
12 button mushrooms (unchopped)
2 bay leaves
½ teaspoonful mixed herbs
1 egg
½ pint double cream
black pepper

Preparation
Roughly chop the duck and/or chicken liver. Chop the onion. Crush the garlic. Line the pate dish with vertical strips of bacon leaving enough length to cover the top. Preheat the oven to number 3-350 degrees.

Method
Melt the butter and fry together the onion, herbs and garlic over a fierce heat. Add the brandy and set alight. When the flames have subsided pour in the red wine and stir for a few moments.
Add the rest of the ingredients except the cream and the egg. Cook gently for ten minutes — take off the heat and stir in the egg and cream. Season with black pepper. The next move is to transfer the mixture into the pate dish which has been previously lined with bacon. Cover the top of the dish with tin foil and place in a roasting tray half filled with water. Bake in a slow oven (number 3-350 degrees) for 1¼ hours. Allow to cool slightly. Place in refrigerator with heavy weights on top to compress the pate. When fully set, turn out and decorate.

HAM and ASPARAGUS QUICHE

A nice alternative to Quiche Lorraine and one of the few really good starters that does not involve fish.

To serve 6

½ onion
4 ounces cooked ham
a knob of butter
4 ounces cheddar cheese
2 eggs
½ pint single cream
black pepper
small tin of asparagus
8 ounces short crust pastry

Preparation
Thinly line an 8 inch flan case with the pastry. Chop the cooked ham. Chop the onion. Grate the cheese. Beat the eggs into the cream. Drain the asparagus. Preheat the oven to number 6-425 degrees.

Method
Cook the onion and ham in butter until the onions are lightly golden. Add in the grated cheese and stir until melted. Remove from the heat and allow to cool slightly before stirring in the egg and cream mixture. Season with black pepper. Arrange the asparagus in the bottom of the flan case with all the tips pointing into the centre. Pour over the mixture whilst still warm. Place in a hot oven (number 6-425 degrees) for 30 minutes or until golden brown. Serve warm, or cold with salad.

HAM and SPINACH PANCAKE

A multi-layered pancake interleaved with spinach and ham and cut like a cake.

Depending on the diameter of the pancake this can serve anything from 6 to 20 people. This recipe is based on a pancake size equal to the average household frying pan, approximately 10 inches, and will produce a dish sufficient to feed 16 people.

THE PANCAKES (10)

8 ounces flour
3 eggs
1 pint milk
2 ounces oil
a pinch of salt

Method
Whisk all ingredients together using half the milk only. Beat until smooth and then add the remaining milk — leave to stand for 30 minutes. Use as required.

Hint. Pancakes will stay fresh for up to 48 hours if stacked on top of one another, interleaved with greaseproof paper, wrapped in a towel and put in the refrigerator.

THE SPINACH AND HAM FILLING

12 ounces cooked ham
2 pounds cooked spinach
4 ounces butter
1 clove of garlic (crushed)
a pinch of nutmeg
salt and black pepper

Preparation
Chop the ham and spinach.

Method
Melt the butter in a pan. Add the ham, spinach, garlic, nutmeg and seasoning. Fry gently for 10 minutes stirring occasionally. Spread the

mixture while still hot over nine of the pancakes before placing one on top of another culminating with the tenth pancake. Press well down and allow two hours to set in a cool place.

Variations

It is equally possible to interleave the pancakes with a mixture of prawns and spinach or even cream cheese beaten up with salami, mortadella sausage and ham.

MUSHROOMS a la GRECQUE

Predominantly button mushrooms with chopped onions and carrots, lightly cooked in a spicy liquor and served chilled.

To serve 4—6

8 ounces button mushrooms
12 small onions
2 raw carrots
1 tomato
1 dessertspoon tomato puree
1 gill of dry white wine
½ pint chicken stock
1 gill olive oil
1 bay leaf
juice of 1 lemon
whole black peppercorns
salt
finely chopped parsley

Preparation
Wipe and quarter the mushrooms. Finely slice the onions and carrots. Peel, seed and chop the tomato.

Method
Place all the ingredients with seasoning in a covered saucepan. Bring to the boil and after a few moments remove from the heat and allow to cool. Take out the bay leaf. Adjust the seasoning. Serve well chilled, sprinkled with parsley. Hot french bread is the finishing touch.

Hints. Resist the temptation to fully cook the vegetables.

POUSSE BEDAINE

Peppers, ham, nuts, onion and cucumber finely chopped and bound together in cream cheese.

To serve 8

1 pound cream cheese
4 ounces cooked ham
1 green pepper
1 sweet red pepper
2 ounces cucumber
1 ounce almonds
½ onion
a pinch of mixed herbs
1 tablespoon of chives

Preparation
Chop finely, ham, peppers, cucumber, almonds, onion, herbs and chives.

Method
Beat the cream cheese until smooth and shining. Gradually introduce all the chopped ingredients and mix well. Pile up in a deep dish and serve with hot thickly cut toast.

Variation
Add prawns to the ingredients given above.

Cook bacon until it is really crisp and crumble it into the cream cheese with fried onions.

PORK CRACKLING
with CIDER DIP

Specifically designed for the man who can never get enough crackling.

pork crackling
oil
salt

1½ pounds cooking apples
1 ounce butter
1 ounce demerara sugar
½ pint rough cider

Preparation
Peel, core and slice the apples. Preheat the oven to number 3-350 degrees.
Score the crackling into long strips and rub with plenty of oil and salt —
take care to remove as much of the pork fat from underneath as possible.

Method
The crackling.
Place the crackling on a baking tray and cook in a slow oven (number 3-
350 degrees) until it is blistered and golden brown all over. During the
cooking baste frequently, draining off excess fat. Remove from the oven.
The crackling will harden and go crisp in two or three minutes. Break
into strips 6 inches long.

Cider dip.
Tip the sliced apples, sugar, butter and cider into a small covered saucepan.
Cook gently until you have achieved an almost smooth apple puree. Pour
into a deep pot, stand on a tray and surround with the strips of pork
crackling.

SALAMI
RATATOUILLE
Salami sausage cut into strips and cooked with Ratatouille.

To serve 4

2 tablespoons oil
1 large onion
2 cloves garlic
3 large courgettes
2 aubergines
2 green peppers
8 large tomatoes
bouquet garni
8 ounces salami
1 glass of dry white wine
salt and black pepper

Preparation
Slice the salami, aubergines, peppers, courgettes and onions. Peel and chop
the tomatoes. Crush the garlic.

Method
Heat the oil in a heavy pan and throw in the onions and garlic. Allow
these to cook until they are brown before adding all the other ingredients
except for the salami and white wine. Gently stir the mixture until the oil
and onions are fully integrated. Add the wine. Cover the pan and stew
slowly, allowing the juices to develop. This should take about 15 minutes
at which point add the salami. Stew a further 15 minutes. Remove the
bouquet garni. Season.

Variation
This is delicious hot, or cold with a little added vinaigrette. Sprinkle
Parmesan if you like.

RED MULLET NICOISE

Red Mullet baked on a bed of green beans, onions, tomatoes and black olives and topped with anchovies and breadcrumbs. This is another fish that you may find difficult to obtain. Try Myall and Sons of Romilly Street, Soho. Telephone 01-437 4063 — if you can buy enough they are usually prepared to send it by passenger train.

To serve 6

12 red mullet (no need to bone, descale or gut)
1 onion
½ pound tomatoes
1 pound cooked french beans
2 green peppers
36 large stoned black olives
1 glass of dry white wine
a sprig of tarragon
2 tablespoons of oil
2 cloves of garlic
36 anchovy fillets
1 cup of fresh white breadcrumbs
salt and black pepper

Preparation
Peel and chop the tomatoes. Slice the green peppers. Slice the onion. Crush the garlic. Preheat the oven to number 7-450 degrees.

Method
Heat the oil in a heavy pan and fry the onions, garlic and peppers until the onions are golden brown. Tip in the wine and tarragon and boil to reduce the quantity by half. Stir in the tomatoes, beans and olives. Season. Now spread the mixture evenly over the bottom of a shallow fireproof dish and arrange the red mullet on top. Finally criss-cross the anchovies over the fish and sprinkle the breadcrumbs liberally over all. Bake in a hot oven (number 7-450 degrees) for 25 minutes — the breadcrumbs should turn a golden brown.

CAULIBIAC of SALMON

One of the most appetizing and sensible ways of cooking salmon, The fish is removed from the bone and layered with thin pancakes each filled with prawns, sweetcorn and peas before being sealed in a thin case of puff pastry. It is baked slowly, sliced up and served with hollandaise sauce.

To serve 4

1½ pounds fresh filleted salmon
3 hard boiled eggs
4 ounces cooked rice
4 ounces prawns
4 ounces cooked mushrooms
4 ounces cooked peas
4 ounces sweet pimento

4 ounces sweetcorn
6 pancakes — see page 28
1½ pound puff pastry
salt and black pepper
1 egg
½ cup of milk

Preparation
Divide the salmon into two equal blocks approximately 8 inches by 5 inches. Chop mushrooms. Chop the hard boiled eggs. Roll out the puff pastry to an oblong 12 inches by 20 inches. Beat the egg and milk together to make an egg wash.

Method
Mix together the rice, chopped mushrooms, peas, pimentos, sweetcorn, chopped hard boiled eggs and prawns. Season. Divide this mixture into six equal parts and roll it up inside the six pancakes.

Assembly
Place half the salmon across the width of the pastry in the centre and lay three of the pancakes in the same direction on top of the salmon.

Repeat this process with the rest of the salmon and the other three pancakes giving you four layers in all.

Dampen the edges of the puff pastry and bring them together completely encasing the salmon. Brush all over with egg wash and place on a baking tray in a moderately hot oven (number 5-400 degrees) for about 40 minutes until the caulibiac is golden brown. Cut into 1½ inch thick slices with a very sharp knife and serve with melted butter or hollandaise sauce.

Hints. To minimise the chance of the caulibiac bursting open, allow it to stand in a cool place for about two hours before baking.

*"Which brings me, dear friends,
to my final point!"*

SALMON, BACON and BANANAS on RICE

This dish is simple to cook and has proved a great favourite at The Hungry Monk.

To serve 1

1 x 8 ounce fresh salmon steak
2 rashers sweet cured back bacon
1 banana
a knob of butter
½ cup of rice
1 cup of water
a pinch of salt
½ clove of garlic
seasoned flour

Preparation
Cook the rice in one cup of water with a pinch of salt. Pass the salmon steak through the seasoned flour.

Method
Melt the butter in a pan and saute the salmon for approximately six minutes on each side until thoroughly cooked. Obviously cooking time will vary with the thickness of the steak. Remove from the pan and keep hot. Slice the banana lengthways and fry in the same pan together with the bacon. Remove these from the pan before finally adding the crushed garlic to the remaining fat in order to fry the rice.

Assembly
Make a bed of the garlic rice. Place the salmon steak in the middle and criss-cross the bacon and bananas over the top. Serve with green salad and french dressing.

☘

Variation
Use boiled rice and serve with hollandaise sauce.

SALMON, BACON and HERBS EN PAPILLOTE

Salmon, bacon and herbs cooked in a sealed tin foil envelope. A wonderful way of retaining all the juices and flavour of fresh salmon.

To serve 1

1 x 8 ounce fresh salmon steak
1 rasher sweet cured back bacon
a sprig of rosemary
a knob of butter
salt and black pepper

Preparation
Preheat the oven to number 7-450 degrees.

Method
Saute the salmon steak in the butter for about two minutes each side. Place the fish on a square sheet of tin foil and cover with the bacon and rosemary. Pour over the melted butter from the pan and season. Bring together the opposite corners of the tin foil to form a triangle and crimp the two edges together, thus forming an air-tight envelope. Cook for 15 minutes in a hot oven (number 7-450 degrees).

Variation
The principle of cooking 'en papillote' can be applied to almost any meat or fish. It is particularly successful with food like salmon, pork and veal where there is a tendency towards dryness.

SEAFOOD PANCAKES

Very thin savoury pancakes filled with prawns, sole, lobster and scallops, coated with a cream and white wine sauce.

To serve 6

1 pound sole, skinned and filleted	juice of two lemons
1½ pound lobster to yield	salt and black pepper
10 ounces of meat	4 ounces butter
6 ounces prawns	½ onion or 4 shallots
10 medium-sized scallops	4 ounces flour
1 large tot of brandy	1 gill of single cream
1 glass of white wine	Parmesan cheese
water	12 pancakes — see page 28
1 bay leaf	

Preparation
Cook the lobster. Remove the meat from the shell and chop into large chunks. Poach the sole and scallops in the white wine, adding water to cover, with the bay leaf, lemon juice and seasoning. Reserve this stock. Chop the onion finely. Preheat oven to number 6-425 degrees.

Method
To make the sauce — melt the butter in a pan and fry the onion until it becomes transparent. Add the flour and stir vigorously. Leave to cook for two or three minutes before adding two pints of the sole and scallop fish stock. Bring to the boil, stirring vigorously, and simmer for 15 minutes. Remove from the heat and after cooling briefly, stir in the cream. Correct the seasoning.

Take the sole and the scallops and chop into small chunks. Add the prawns and the lobster meat. Pour the brandy into a small saucepan — heat and flambe. Before the flames die down, quickly pour it over the fish.

Combine the fish, together with any remaining brandy, with half the sauce. Reserve the rest.

Assembly
Half an hour before eating the dish divide the mixture between the 12 pancakes, roll them up tightly and lay in a shallow fireproof dish. Coat with the remainder of the sauce and sprinkle with Parmesan. Place in a hot oven (number 6-425 degrees) for ten minutes or until thoroughly heated.

Hints. See Ham and Spinach Pancakes on page 28.

Variations

In the event of lobster being out of season or too expensive, use the white meat of crab or even fresh mussels.

*"You don't have to love me <u>all</u> the time
Brother Anthony!"*

BROCHETTE of SOLE and SCALLOPS

A delicious fish kebab served with paprika rice.

To serve 6

12 x 4 ounce fillets of sole
12 large scallops
48 large field mushrooms
3 ounces melted butter
2 cups of rice
1 dessertspoon paprika
1 clove of garlic
a sprig of fresh fennel
a pinch of oregano
2 lemons

Preparation
Skin the sole. Remove stalks and lightly fry the mushrooms. Crush the garlic. Cook the rice with the paprika and garlic in 4 cups of water. Separate the orange tongues from the scallops. Chop the fennel. Light the grill.

Method
Cut each fillet of sole into two pieces — both of which should be folded. Now push the various ingredients alternately on to the skewers — sole, mushroom, scallop, mushroom and so on. Finally sprinkle over the fennel and oregano before brushing with butter and positioning under the grill on a baking tray. Grill for ten minutes, turning the skewer frequently. Serve on a bed of the paprika rice with wedges of lemon.

Variation
Rolls of crispy bacon can be used to replace the scallops — very tasty.

CASSOULET of SOLE

Fillets of sole set in an individual open pastry case and covered with mushrooms and prawns in a cream and white wine sauce.

To serve 6

6 x 4 inch pastry cases baked blind
12 x 4 ounce fillets of Dover sole
12 ounces prawns
36 button mushrooms
½ pint of dry white wine
½ an onion

1 bay leaf
juice of a lemon
1 pint of double cream
4 egg yolks
salt and white pepper

Preparation
Skin the sole. Fry the mushrooms in butter. Preheat the oven to number 3-350 degrees.

Method
Roll the fillets of sole and place them, tightly packed, in an oven dish. Pour over the white wine, add the bay leaf, onion, lemon juice and seasoning. Bake in a slow oven number 3-350 degrees covered with buttered paper until the sole are cooked. Remove the fish, drain them well and arrange two fillets in each pastry case together with the prawns and mushrooms. Keep warm. Strain the remaining fish stock into a heavy frying pan and reduce to ½ pint. Allow the fish stock to cool slightly.

Meanwhile, in a separate bowl beat the egg yolks and gradually add the double cream to form an emulsion. Take a small whisk and very slowly pour the emulsion into the now cooling stock, beating all the time. When the eggs, cream and stock are thoroughly blended, return the pan to a medium flame and, whisking all the time, bring the sauce to a point just short of boiling. Do not on any account boil. You should now have a delicious thick creamy sauce that only requires a touch of seasoning before it is ready to be poured over the fillets of sole. Finally flash the cassoulets under a hot grill to slightly brown — serve immediately.

Hint. To minimise the possibility of disaster that occurs if you allow the emulsion of cream, eggs and stock to boil, it is considerably safer to do this part of the operation in a double saucepan.

Variation
Try putting a bit of spinach in each pastry case underneath the fillets of sole.

TROUT BOURGUIGNONNE

Trout cooked in red wine, with ham and mushrooms.

To serve 6

6 large fresh river trout —
   gutted
½ bottle of strong red wine
24 button onions
24 button mushrooms
2 thick slices of mild cooked ham
½ cup of oil
½ onion
1 carrot

1 stick celery
½ lemon
salt and black pepper
3 ounces flour
1 dessertspoon of tomato puree
1½ pints of fish stock
1 bay leaf
1 bouquet garni
chopped parsley

Preparation

Chop up the ham into cubes. Peel the button onions. Wipe the mushrooms. Preheat the oven to number 5-400 degrees.

Method

To make the sauce — heat the oil in a saucepan and chop in the carrot, celery, onion and the lemon. Add the bay leaf and seasoning and cook until the onion is golden. Stir in the flour and cook for five minutes before adding the tomato puree. Cook for five more minutes and then gently pour in the fish stock and bring to the boil, stirring continuously. Simmer gently for 20 minutes with the addition of a bouquet garni. Add a little gravy browning to give you a dark, rich looking sauce.

While the sauce is simmering, the trout should be arranged in a shallow fireproof dish well buttered. Pour in all the wine and sprinkle the ham, mushrooms and button onions over the fish. Cover with lightly oiled greaseproof paper and poach in a moderately hot oven (number 5-400 degrees) for 15—20 minutes.

Ideally the trout and the brown sauce will finish cooking at the same time.

Now all you have to do is strain the brown sauce over the trout endeavouring to mix the red wine and the brown sauce as thoroughly as possible without disturbing the fish.

Put the dish back in the oven for another five minutes and serve sprinkled with finely chopped parsley.

FILLET of BEEF WELLINGTON

By no means unique to The Hungry Monk but undoubtedly our favourite way of cooking fillet steak.

To serve 8

1 x 4 pound fillet of prime Scotch beef
2 ounces butter
24 big field mushrooms
12 rashers of streaky bacon
1½ pounds puff pastry
1 egg
½ cup of milk
black pepper

Preparation
Trim the fat and sinew off the fillet. Saute the mushrooms in butter till soft. Beat the egg and milk together to make the egg wash. Preheat the oven to number 7-450 degrees.

Method
Firstly fold the mignon (pointed end) of the fillet under the tournedos (middle of the fillet) so that the fillet has approximately the same girth throughout. Sprinkle liberally with black pepper.

Roll out the puff pastry to a square sufficient to encase the entire fillet. Position the fillet in the centre of the puff pastry and wrap it on all sides with the bacon and mushrooms. Dampen all four edges of the puff pastry — wrap and seal. Brush with egg wash and bake in a hot oven (number 7-450 degrees) for 45 minutes to one hour, depending on how rare you like your beef.

Variations
The substitution of liver pate for bacon and mushrooms in Beef Wellington is a pleasant change.

KEBAB en CROUTE

A skewer laden with chunks of rump steak dressed with pate and wrapped in puff pastry.

To serve 4

1½ pounds rump steak
4 ounces liver pate — (see page 26)
1 pound puff pastry
oil
salt and black pepper
1 egg
½ cup of milk
4 skewers

Preparation

Cut up the steak into large chunks. Beat the egg and milk together to make the egg wash. Preheat the oven to number 8-475 degrees.

Method

Take the cubes of beef and toss them into a frying pan of hot oil to seal but not to cook. Season. Remove and push them onto the skewers. Set aside. Roll out the puff pastry as thinly as possible to a size sufficient to encase the steak while still allowing both ends of the skewer to protrude. Place the skewer, laden with the steak, in the centre of the puff pastry and distribute one ounce of pate evenly along the length of each kebab. Dampen the edges of the pastry, wrap and seal. Place on a baking tray, the join in the pastry facing downwards. Brush with the egg wash and bake in a very hot oven (number 8-475 degrees) for 15 to 20 minutes depending on how rare you like the steak.

Variation

Here are some other ideas for kebabs en croute. In each case cook in much the same way as the beef kebab shown above. Pork, prune and apple. Lamb and dried apricots. Veal, ham and gruyere cheese.

MEDALLIONS of BEEF in WHITE WINE SAUCE

Small thick slices of fillet steak cooked rare and served with a rich white wine and mushroom sauce.

To serve 6

18 x ½ inch thick slices of fillet steak
2 ounces butter
1 onion
2 green peppers
8 ounces button mushrooms

2 tots of brandy
½ bottle of dry white wine
1 pint double cream
1 bay leaf
salt and black pepper

Preparation
Season both sides of the steaks. Slice the green peppers, mushrooms and onion.

Method
Take the medallions of beef and fry them in butter in a very hot pan for one minute each side or longer depending on your taste for rare steak. Transfer to a serving dish and keep warm. Using the pan in which the steak has been cooked, toss in the mushrooms, peppers and onion and cook until soft. Flambe with the brandy and add the white wine. Cook on a fierce flame for five minutes to reduce by half.

Pour the double cream into the reduction of the wine and vegetables — stir for a moment. Add the bay leaf, bring to the boil, simmer for 10 minutes adjusting the seasoning as you do so. Pour over the waiting medallions and serve immediately.

Hint. You may prefer a less rich sauce with your medallions than the one made with pure cream described above. The following cream sauce is a very satisfactory alternative and should be added instead of one pint of double cream to the reduction of wine and vegetables.

To make this cream sauce — Melt one ounce of butter in a saucepan and add one tablespoon of flour. Cook for a few minutes before adding ½ pint of milk, salt and white pepper and a bay leaf, finish with ½ pint of double cream and bringing quickly to the boil. Simmer for 10—15 minutes.

RARE BEEF PANCAKES

A slice of rare sirloin steak rolled in a pancake with liver pate
and eaten with red wine sauce.

To serve 8

3 pounds of boned, trimmed sirloin of beef
8 pancakes — see page 28
1 pound of liver pate — see page 26
dripping
a clove of garlic
salt and pepper

THE SAUCE
1 ounce butter
6 ounces mushrooms
6 ounces tomatoes
1 onion
1 tot of brandy
1 glass of white wine
1 pint of espagnole sauce — see page 49
a clove of garlic

Preparation
Make the pancakes and keep warm. Preheat the oven to number 6-425
degrees. Put the pate in a warm place. Wipe and chop the mushrooms. Skin
and chop the tomatoes. Peel and chop the onion. Crush the garlic.

Method
Roast the beef with one clove of crushed garlic in an open roasting tray
having first seasoned it with salt and black pepper and dotted it with
dripping. Depending on how rare you like your beef, cook for anything
between 35 minutes and one hour. Meanwhile melt the butter in a pan and
cook the onion and garlic till brown. Toss in the tomatoes and mushrooms
and continue frying until soft. Add brandy and flambe. Pour in the white
wine and reduce by half. Add the espagnole sauce, stirring slowly until
everything is piping hot. Cover the pan and simmer gently.

Assembly
A few minutes before serving the dish, carve the steak into 16 slices, and
lay two on each pancake together with two ounces of pate. Roll up and
quickly pour the red wine sauce over. Eat Immediately.

"It's the ordinary sinful little
things that make life worth living!"

ESPAGNOLE SAUCE

A great many of the dishes that follow in the book are made using this delicious sauce as a base.

To make 1 quart

4 ounces good dripping
2 ounces diced carrot
2 ounces diced onion
2 ounces diced celery
some mushroom stalks
1 ounce chopped fat bacon
4 ounces flour
1 large tablespoon of tomato puree
1 tablespoon of Worcester sauce
1 bay leaf
bouquet garni
2½ pints good brown meat stock

Method

Melt the dripping in a saucepan and fry the carrot, onion, celery, mushroom stalks and bacon until golden brown. Then tip in the flour and continue to cook for two or three minutes, stirring briskly. Gradually pour in the stock, bring to the boil and simmer for ten minutes. Now add the tomato puree, Worcester sauce, the bouquet garni and the bay leaf and allow to bubble gently for a further ten minutes. Adjust the seasoning and add gravy browning if necessary.

The next move is to reduce the sauce by about half a pint which can be done in two ways. Either rest a piece of greaseproof paper on the surface of the sauce and cook in a low oven for one hour, or if time is short, cook uncovered over a low flame for about half an hour.

Strain into a jug ready for use.

OUR FAVOURITE WAYS of COOKING STEAK

Asparagus and Gruyere Cheese

Cook the steak in the normal way and while still hot lay three or four sticks of asparagus over the top and cover with a slice of gruyere cheese. Flash under the grill. Garnish with watercress.

Anchovies and Stuffed Olives

Cook the steak in the normal way and while still hot criss-cross the anchovy fillets over the top placing a thin slice of stuffed olive in each diamond. Flash under the grill.

Horseradish Butter

Take four ounces of butter and mix it with a dessertspoon of freshly grated horseradish. Roll into a sausage shape, wrap in tin foil and chill. Cook the steak in the normal way and just before serving, slice the horseradish butter over the top.

Anchovy, Garlic and Parsley Butter

Take three anchovy fillets, one clove of garlic, a pinch of parsley and pound together. Blend thoroughly with 4 ounces of butter and roll into a sausage shape, wrap in tin foil and chill. Cook the steak in the normal way and just before serving, slice the butter over the top.

Ratatouille

1 large aubergine	2 cloves of garlic
2 green peppers	1 glass of dry white wine
2 courgettes	4 tablespoons of oil
1 onion	salt and black pepper
8 tomatoes	

Method — Slice all the vegetables and toss into a pan with the exception of the tomatoes. Cook briefly with the oil and crushed garlic. Add the tomatoes and white wine. Season, cover and allow to stew for half an hour.

Assembly — Cook the steak in the normal way and serve on a bed of the ratatouille.

Raw Onion, Beer and Cheese

Take two — three ounces grated Cheddar cheese, a pinch of cayenne pepper and cook together with ¼ bottle of Guinness per person until the cheese is quite melted.

Meanwhile cook the steak in the normal way and thinly slice raw onion over the top. Scoop the melted cheese and beer mixture over the onions and flash the whole thing under the grill till golden brown.

The Hungry Monk, please.... on Polegate 2178.
No, No — POLEGATE   P for Pharaoh,
O for Obadiah, L for Leviticus, E for
   Ezekiel....

CHICKEN PANCAKES

The first dish that we ever cooked at The Hungry Monk and still one of the most popular. Very thin pancakes filled with chicken in a cream and white wine sauce with mushrooms.

To serve 4

8 pancakes — see page 28	4 ounces butter
1 x 3 pound chicken	8 ounces mushrooms
1 onion	4 ounces flour
1 carrot	1 glass of white wine
1 bay leaf	1 gill of double cream
1 bouquet garni	Parmesan cheese
salt	salt and white pepper

Preparation
Make the pancakes. Wipe and slice the mushrooms. Poach the chicken in a large pot with the onion, carrot, bay leaf, bouquet garni and salt in enough water to cover, for one hour. Remove the chicken from stock and allow to cool — reserve the stock. Preheat the oven to number 6-425 degrees.

Method
Melt the butter in a saucepan, add the mushrooms and fry for a moment or two. Add the flour, stir and continue to cook for two or three minutes before gradually pouring in 1½ pints of the strained chicken stock. Bring to the boil and allow to simmer for a further 10—15 minutes. Remove from the heat and allow to cool slightly before blending in the cream with the white wine. Adjust the seasoning.

Now to the chicken — pull the meat off the bird and chop into decent sized chunks. All that remains is to pour the sauce over the chicken — stirring slowly as you do so until the chicken meat is well bound. Resist the temptation to use too much sauce and keep at least one pint in reserve.

Half an hour before eating the dish, spoon the chicken mixture onto the pancakes, roll them up tightly and place in a shallow fireproof dish. Coat with the remainder of the sauce and sprinkle with Parmesan. Then bake in a hot oven (number 6-425 degrees) for ten minutes or until thoroughly heated.

Hint. Pancakes will stay fresh for up to 48 hours if stacked on top of one another, interleaved with greasproof paper and wrapped in a tea towel and put in the refrigerator.

Variation

These pancakes are delicious with a lemon and tarragon sauce. In this case simply add the juice of three lemons and some sprigs of fresh tarragon at the same time as pouring in the stock

AMERICAN CHICKEN PIE

Chicken with pimentos, sweetcorn and chopped hard boiled egg, covered with a puff pastry crust.

To serve 6

1 x 3 pound chicken	4 hard boiled eggs
1 onion	2 sweet red pimentos
1 carrot	4 ounces cooked peas
1 bay leaf	a small tin of sweetcorn
1 bouquet garni	1 pound puff pastry
salt	1 egg
2 ounces butter	½ cup of milk
2 ounces flour	salt and white pepper

Preparation

Beat the egg and milk together to make an egg wash. Peel and chop the hard boiled eggs. Chop the pimentos. Preheat the oven to number 7-450 degrees. Poach the chicken in a large pot with the onion, carrot, bay leaf, bouquet garni and salt, in enough water to cover, for one hour. Remove the chicken from the stock and allow to cool. Reserve the stock.

Method

Melt the butter in a saucepan, add the pimentos and fry for a moment or two. Then add the flour, stir and continue to cook for two or three minutes, before gradually pouring in one pint of the strained chicken stock. Bring to the boil and allow to bubble for a few seconds. Remove from the heat and add the peas, sweetcorn and chopped hard boiled eggs. Adjust the seasoning. Allow to stand while you remove the chicken meat from the bone and chop into half inch chunks. Now tip this chopped chicken meat into the pimento sauce — stir and transfer the whole mixture into a fairly deep pie dish.

Roll out the puff pastry and lay it over the top of the pie dish, trimming the edges with a sharp knife and brushing the surface with egg wash. The uncooked pie will keep in good condition in a refrigerator for up to two days. Finally bake in a hot oven (number 7-450 degrees) for 30 minutes or until the pastry is golden brown.

Hints. This dish is an excellent candidate for the freezer.

Variations

Try making this pie with turkey and oysters — a very useful way of using up cold turkey.

ROAST DUCK with BLACK CHERRY SAUCE

Still our favourite way of serving duck.

To serve 4

1 x 4 pound duck (cleaned weight)

salt
1 pint espagnole sauce — see page 49
1 small tin of pitted black cherries
2 tablespoons of redcurrant jelly
2 tablespoons of Worcester sauce
1 glass of red wine
1 tot of brandy

Preparation
Preheat the oven to number 8-475 degrees.

Method.
To roast the duck
Firstly prick the duck **all over** with a sharp fork to release the grease from under the skin during cooking, rub well with salt to help the skin go really crisp. Place in a roasting tray with no fat, set in the middle of the oven and cook for 1¼ hours, basting at regular intervals. The duck is cooked when the skin is a dark golden brown all over.

Lift the duck out of the roasting tray and keep warm. Tip away the duck fat leaving just the meat juices in the bottom of the roasting tray.

To make the Black Cherry Sauce
Place the roasting tray, still containing the duck juices over a low flame and pour in the brandy. Flambe. Add the black cherries with a little of their juice, Worcester sauce, redcurrant jelly and the wine and stir briskly for five minutes allowing the liquor to reduce by a quarter. Now pour in one pint of espagnole sauce. Stir thoroughly for a minute or two and serve separately with the duck. ✿

Hints. Take care not to pour the black cherry sauce over the duck as it will turn the crisp skin soggy. It is worth paying a bit extra and getting a good fresh free range duck with plenty of meat on it.

ROAST DUCKLING with TURNIPS

In contrast to the more traditional fruit sauces, turnips have a rare savoury quality when eaten with duck.

To serve 4

1 x 4 pound duck (cleaned weight)
salt
4 medium-sized turnips
1 large Spanish onion
1 glass of red wine
1 pint espagnole sauce — see page 49

Preparation
Peel and slice the turnips and onion. Preheat the oven to number 8-475 degrees.

Method
As with our previous recipe for roast duck, start by pricking the bird all over and rubbing it with salt. Place in a roasting tray without any fat and cook for 20 minutes. Lift the tray out of the oven and arrange the sliced onion and turnips around the bird. Give the duck and vegetables a thorough basting and replace in the oven for a further hour, basting occasionally. When the duck is cooked remove it from the roasting tray and keep warm.

Drain the fat from the vegetables in the roasting tray, retaining the meat juices. Pour in the red wine and bring to the boil over a strong flame. Allow to simmer for ten minutes.

Lastly pour the espagnole sauce into the liquor and stir gently, taking care not to break up the vegetables. Cook for a minute or two until heated through and serve with the duck.

Hint. As with Black Cherry Sauce resist the temptation to pour the Turnip Sauce over the duck, making the skin go soggy.

DUCK, APPLE and SAGE PANCAKES

These are the most recent addition to the long tradition of The Hungry Monk pancakes. What you lose in the crispness of roast duck is more than made up for in added succulence.

To serve 5

1 x 4 pound roasted duck (cleaned weight) — see page 55
2 medium cooking apples
1 dessertspoon of demerara sugar
1 knob of butter
2 good pinches of dried sage or 6 leaves of freshly chopped sage
½ pint espagnole sauce
10 pancakes — see page 28

For the Cheese Sauce
2 ounces butter
2 ounces flour
1 pint milk
1 small onion covered with a bay leaf and studded with cloves
4 ounces Cheddar cheese
salt

Preparation
Roast the duck in the manner described on page 55. Peel and chop the apples. Grate the cheese finely. Preheat the oven to number 6-425 degrees.

Method
Remove the meat from the duck while the bird is still warm, chop into half inch chunks and set aside.
Melt the butter and add the apple, sage and sugar. Cook slowly until the apple softens before tipping in the chopped duck meat. Finally pour the espagnole sauce gently into the saucepan and stir. Set to one side.

The Cheese Sauce
Melt the butter, add the flour and cook for two or three minutes before whisking in the milk and salt. Put in the onion cloute and bring briefly to the boil before allowing to simmer for ten minutes. Remove the onion and throw in the grated cheese. Continue to stir over a low heat until the cheese has melted.

Assembly

Half an hour before serving the dish, spoon the duck, apple and sage mixture onto each pancake, roll up tightly and place in a shallow fireproof dish. Coat with the cheese sauce previously prepared and bake in a hot oven (number 6-425 degrees) for 15 minutes.

"In fact, if it wasn't for the Grace of God, we'd be having rather a good time!"

GAME
CASSOULET

Our version of a classic French dish from Languedoc where various game are interleaved with haricot beans and vegetables and baked with a crisp topping of breadcrumbs.

To serve 6

4 breasts of pheasant	2 Spanish onions
6 breasts of pigeon	12 tomatoes
12 thin slices of salami	8 ounces pork fat
12 slices of lean pork	2 cloves of garlic
12 rashers of streaky bacon	salt and black pepper
1 pound dried haricot beans	a pinch of sage, marjoram and thyme
4 carrots	breadcrumbs

Preparation
Soak the haricot beans in water overnight. Slice the breasts of pheasant into small escalopes. Slice the carrots and onions. Skin and chop the tomatoes. Cut the pork fat into lardons. Crush the garlic. Combine the herbs with the breadcrumbs. Preheat the oven to number 4-375 degrees.

Method
Take an uncovered saucepan and scoop into it the chopped, carrots, onions and tomatoes, with the pork fat, haricot beans, garlic and seasoning. Add water to cover, bring sharply to the boil and allow to simmer for half an hour — set aside.

Take an oval casserole and butter well. The idea now is to place alternate layers of the bean and vegetable mixture and the various meats, starting with a layer of pheasant, pigeon, salami, bacon and pork, and finishing with a very top layer of the beans and vegetables. Sprinkle generously with the breadcrumb mixture. Place in a moderate oven (number 4-375 degrees) for 1 hour.

Hint. This is a good freezer dish.

Variation
In the absence of game; duck, pork and salami sausage make a good substitute.

PIGEON en CROUTE

Breasts of pigeon cooked with liver pate and a rich red wine sauce wrapped in a crisp parcel of puff pastry.

To serve 4

THE PIGEON	PIGEON SAUCE
4 young plump tender pigeons	1 onion
4 ounces mushrooms	1 carrot
2 ounces butter	1 stick of celery
1 pint mussels	1 bay leaf
1 large glass of port	a sprig of tarragon
1 pound puff pastry	1 bouquet garni
1 egg	1 tablespoon Worcester sauce
½ cup of milk	1 tablespoon wine vinegar
salt and black pepper	1 ounce tomato puree
	2 ounces butter
	2 ounces flour
	salt and black pepper

Preparation

Remove the breasts from the raw pigeons, season and marinade in the port. Chop the remaining pigeon carcasses. Prepare the mussels and remove from their shells in the way described on page 18. Wipe and slice the mushrooms. Chop the onion, carrot and celery. Beat the egg and milk together to make the egg wash. Preheat the oven to number 6-425 degrees.

Method

Take a large pan and throw in the chopped pigeon carcasses, bay leaf, tarragon, bouquet garni, onion, carrot, celery Worcester sauce and wine vinegar. Cover with water, bring to the boil and simmer, covered, for one and a half hours. Strain into a smaller pan and boil rapidly to reduce to one pint.

In a separate pan, melt the butter, add the flour and cook for a few minutes before adding the tomato puree and the pint of pigeon stock. Bring briskly to the boil and allow to simmer for ten minutes.

Turning our attention to the pigeon, lift the breasts out of the marinade and fry with the mushrooms in butter. After five minutes pour in the port in which the pigeon breasts have been marinading, and allow to bubble until the port has reduced by half. All that remains is to pour the pigeon sauce into this pan together with the mussels and blend thoroughly. Allow to go quite cold.

You are now ready to roll out four pastry squares 6 inches by 10 inches and place two pigeon breasts in the centre of each. Spoon the cold sauce over the breasts and, dampening the outer edges of the pastry, wrap and seal. Brush with egg wash. Allow to stand in a cool place for one hour or so before baking in a hot oven (number 6-425 degrees) for 20 minutes.

Hint. Try not to get any of the pigeon sauce onto the edge of the pastry, as it will make it difficult to achieve a perfect seal.

"When you've finished renouncing the flesh and the Devil, Abbot says, would you please help with the potatoes!"

HOT GAME PIE

An English classic.

To serve 8

1 pheasant	3 ounces butter
1 grouse	3 ounces flour
1 partridge	1 tablespoon of tomato puree
1 saddle of hare	1 teaspoonful of English mustard
8 ounces of rump steak	1 large glass of marsala
24 button mushrooms	1 tablespoon of Worcester sauce
1 pound cooked ham	1½ pound puff pastry
1 onion	1 egg
1 carrot	½ cup of milk
1 bay leaf	salt and black pepper
1 bouquet garni	

Preparation

Remove the breasts and legs from the pheasant, grouse and partridge and chop roughly.

Bone the saddle of hare and cut up the meat.

Finally chop the rump steak into large chunks, and the ham into small cubes.

Now place all the chopped game, mushrooms, ham and steak into a bowl, season and set aside. Preheat the oven to number 5-400 degrees.

Make a good rich game stock by putting all the bones and carcasses into a large pot with the onion, carrot, bay leaf and bouquet garni and stewing, with water to cover, for one and a half hours.

Beat the egg and milk together to make the egg wash.

Method

Take a large heavy saucepan and melt the butter. Toss in the chopped game, steak, ham and mushrooms and brown on all sides. Stir in the flour and cook for two or three minutes. Spoon in the tomato puree and mustard. Allow to sizzle gently while you measure one and a half pints of the reduced game stock. Pour this in, bring to the boil and simmer for ten minutes. While this is happening stir in the marsala and Worcester sauce. Correct the seasoning and colouring.

All that remains is to transfer the meat into a suitably-sized pie dish. Roll out the puff pastry and drape it over the top, remembering to dampen the edges of the pie dish as you do so. It may be necessary, depending on the dimensions of the pie dish, to support the pie crust in the centre with a pie bird. Brush with egg wash. Place in a moderately hot oven (number 4-375 degrees) for one hour till the pastry is crisp and golden.

*"I just couldn't bring myself
to do it!"*

LAMB WELLINGTON

A piece of English lamb filled with lemon stuffing and wrapped in puff pastry.

To serve 4

THE LAMB
One loin of English lamb without the chump — ask the butcher to remove the bone
8 rashers of streaky bacon
1 pound of puff pastry
1 egg and ½ cup of milk

THE LEMON STUFFING
6 ounces of white breadcrumbs
2 lemons
a pinch of rosemary
1 ounce of butter
½ onion
salt and black pepper

Preparation
Chop the onion. Grate the zest and squeeze the juice of the lemons. Beat the egg and milk together to make the egg wash. Trim excess fat from the lamb. Preheat the oven to number 6-425 degrees.

Method
Firstly the lemon stuffing. Melt the butter in a saucepan with the onions and rosemary. Cook for five minutes before sprinkling in the lemon zest and juice, together with the breadcrumbs. Stir thoroughly with a wooden spoon adding salt and pepper as required. You should now have a stuffing that is stiff in consistency and tasting strongly of lemon and rosemary.

Next, roll out the pastry into a piece large enough to encase the lamb. Take the lamb and place it on the table fat downwards. Lay the bacon across the top of the meat, and, making a roll of the stuffing, place this parallel to the eye of the meat. Finally roll the lamb so that its edges just meet and place it, join downward, in the middle of the pastry. Dampen the edges of the pastry, wrap and seal. Place on a baking tray, brush with egg wash and cook in a hot oven (number 6-425 degrees) for 45 minutes.

Variations
Pate can be used instead of lemon stuffing although there is a danger that it will overpower the flavour of the lamb.

BEST END of LAMB with PORT, ORANGE and REDCURRANT SAUCE

A delicious combination of the tenderest part of the lamb and a crispy savoury coating, prevented from being too rich by a sharp fruity sauce.

To serve 2
THE LAMB

One best end of English lamb —
  ask the butcher to remove
  the chine
2 ounces of breadcrumbs
1 clove of garlic
2 anchovy fillets

a pinch of rosemary
a pinch of thyme
a pinch of oregano
seasoned flour
1 egg
a little milk

THE SAUCE
a wine glass of port
2 oranges
2 tablespoons of redcurrant jelly

Preparation

Pound the herbs, garlic and anchovies together to a puree and rub into the breadcrumbs.

Trim excess fat from the lamb — remove the tip of the blade bone to facilitate carving.

Beat the egg and the milk together to make an egg wash.

Carefully peel the zest only from the oranges (not the pith) and shred it finely. Remove the pith from the oranges and fillet the segments. Preheat the oven to number 6-425 degrees.

Method

Firstly take the lamb and, placing it on the table bones down, sprinkle the entire joint with flour. Follow this with a good thick coating of egg wash. Pat the savoury anchovy and breadcrumb mixture onto the sticky egg washed surface of the lamb and place in a hot oven (number 6-425 degrees) for 30—45 minutes, depending on the size of the joint until brown and crispy.

The sauce is simply made. The redcurrant jelly, orange zest and segments and port should be combined in a small saucepan and gently cooked until hot.

To serve, either cut the best end in half, and hand the sauce separately (which is the way we recommend) or slice into individual chops.

65

"I'm not a believer really. I only
joined for the social side!"

LAMB KEBABS with BARBECUE SAUCE

Chunks of English lamb interleaved with mushrooms, green peppers and tomatoes, and grilled on a skewer.

To serve 4

THE KEBAB
24 x 1 ounce chunks cut from the large
   end of a leg of English lamb
24 button mushrooms
4 green peppers
6 firm tomatoes
salt and black pepper
Worcester sauce
2 tablespoons of oil
4 long skewers

THE SAUCE
2 tablespoons of mango chutney
1 tablespoon of Worcester
   sauce
1 small knob of butter
1 onion
a pinch of cayenne
a sprig of tarragon
1 pint espagnole sauce

Preparation
Lay the lamb on a board and liberally sprinkle with salt, black pepper and Worcester sauce. Cut up the green peppers into 1 inch squares. Cut the tomatoes in half. Wipe the mushrooms. Peel and chop the onion finely.

Method
It is first necessary to seal the lamb, green peppers and mushrooms. Heat the oil in a pan to smoking heat and toss in the cubes of lamb, turning them briskly until all the sides are sealed and brown. Remove immediately, allow oil to regain heat and repeat the process with the green peppers and mushrooms. Push all these ingredients including the tomatoes alternately onto the skewers. Place on a baking sheet ready for grilling.

To make the sauce, heat the butter in a pan and add the onion, Worcester sauce, mango chutney, cayenne pepper and tarragon. Heat through well and pour in the espagnole sauce. Stir, bringing to the boil and allow to simmer for five minutes. Transfer the sauce into a fireproof jug and keep hot. Grill the kebabs for approximately ten minutes under a hot grill, turning once.

Serve with plain boiled rice or vegetables and hand the sauce separately.

LAMB STEAK with CREAM and CURRY SAUCE

This must be young English lamb and the steak taken from the large end of the leg.

To serve 4

4 lamb steaks 1 inch thick
2 tablespoons of oil
4 slices of brown bread
1 clove of garlic
2 dessertspoons of mango chutney
8 ounces almonds

½ onion
2 dessertspoons of curry powder
1 small cooking apple
½ pint double cream — soured
salt
watercress to garnish

Preparation
Crush the garlic. Cut the bread into rounds the same size as the lamb steaks. Finely chop the onion, cooking apple and the almonds before mixing together with the chutney and garlic in a large bowl. Season both sides of the steaks.

Method
Cook the lamb steaks in the hot oil to your own taste — we recommend them to be slightly pink in the middle. Having done this remove the steaks from the pan and keep warm in the oven. Tip the curry powder into the frying pan with the lamb fat and stir over a medium flame for two or three minutes, before emptying in the bowl of chopped almonds, etc. Cook for a moment or two and fold in the cream. Bring briefly to the boil and allow to simmer for five or ten minutes, adding salt as necessary.

While the sauce is simmering pour a little fresh oil into a new pan, heat to smoking point and fry the bread until crisp on both sides. Transfer the croutes to a hot serving dish, position the lamb steaks on top. Spoon over a thick coating of the curry sauce, garnish with watercress and speed to the dining table.

PORK and PATE
WELLINGTON

PORK

Loin of pork stuffed with liver pate and baked slowly in puff pastry.

To serve 6

3 pounds of loin of pork cut from the thick end complete with kidney and
   fillet. Ask the butcher to remove the bone.
8 ounces liver pate — see page 26
1½ pounds puff pastry
1 egg
½ cup of milk

Preparation
Trim the skin and fat from the pork. Discard the fat. Score the skin and rub
well with plenty of salt.

Remove the kidney, chop finely and mix well with the pate.

Beat the egg and milk together to make the egg wash.

Preheat the oven to number 4-375 degrees.

Method
Roll out the puff pastry to an oblong large enough to completely encase
the joint of pork.

In order to stuff the pork — place the joint flat on the table and distribute
the pate along its length before wrapping the meat around it. Place join
downwards in the middle of the puff pastry. Now dampen all four edges of
the pastry, wrap and seal. Transfer to a baking tray, brush with the egg
wash, loosely cover with a sheet of tin foil and cook in a moderate oven
(number 4-375 degrees) for one and a half hours.

After 45 minutes remove the tin foil to brown the pastry. At this point put
the pork skin into the top of the oven on a baking tray.

Serve the pork and pate Wellington cut into thick slices and accompanied
by strips of crackling.

Cooking "en croute" in this way has the tremendous advantage of keeping
the meat succulent — for this reason we do not recommend an accompanying
sauce. Instead serve with juicy vegetables like celery provencale (see page
79), Petit Pois a la Francais (see page 79) or Green Salad.

PORK CHOP en PAPILLOTE

Pork sealed in tin foil with mushrooms and sour cream.

To serve 4

4 pork chops
4 1 foot square pieces of foil
24 button mushrooms
a pinch of sage
a pinch of thyme
a pinch of marjoram
4 tablespoons of thick sour cream
a dash of oil

Preparation
Preheat the oven to number 7-450 degrees. Skin and trim the fat from the chops.

Method
It is first necessary to seal the pork chops in very hot oil on both sides until nicely browned. Lift out of the pan, drain and allow to cool.

For each pork chop take a sheet of foil and place a chop on it. Cover with mushrooms, sprinkle with the herbs and dollop with sour cream before bringing together the opposite corners of the foil and sealing the edges to form an airtight triangular parcel. Place on a baking tray and cook in hot oven (number 7-450 degrees) for 20 minutes.

Variation
As we have said earlier in this book, cooking "en papillote" has endless possibilities with particular application to those meats with a tendency to dryness like pork and veal, breast of chicken and turkey.

PORK CHOPS STUFFED with PRUNES and CHESTNUTS

A fairly simple way of giving a straight forward pork chop a bit of a lift.

To serve 2

THE PORK CHOPS
2 thick pork chops
4 chestnuts (tinned or dried)
6 prunes
1 tablespoon of oil
salt and black pepper
chopped parsley

THE RED WINE SAUCE
1 large glass of red wine
¾ pint espagnole sauce
(see page 49).

Preparation
If using dried prunes and chestnuts soak overnight. Stone the prunes. Trim the skin and fat from the chops. Preheat the oven to number 3-350 degrees.

Method
Take the chops and lay them flat on the table. With a sharp pointed knife make a deep incision from the side through the fat and the eye of the meat to the bone. You should be satisfied that you have made a pocket large enough to enable you to stuff the chops with the prunes and chestnuts. Season the chops on both sides and fry for 15 minutes turning once.

Transfer to a small fireproof serving dish and keep hot in a low oven, reserving the meat juices in the frying pan.

Pour in the red wine and bring sharply to the boil. Allowing to simmer sufficiently to reduce the wine by half. Now pour in ¾ pint of espagnole sauce and heat through. Pour this over the cooked chops and return them to the oven, increasing the heat to number 6-425 degrees, for ten minutes. Garnish with chopped parsley.

Variation
One alternative is to stuff the pork chops with ham and make the sauce with dry sherry rather than red wine.

PAUPIETTES of VEAL

Little parcels of veal filled with a savoury stuffing and cooked in a cream and sherry sauce.

To serve 4

4 x 6 ounce escalopes of veal beaten thin

THE STUFFING	THE SAUCE
a knob of butter	2 ounces butter
½ onion	8 ounces mushrooms
a pinch of basil	½ onion
a pinch of rosemary	1 ounce flour
2 fillets of anchovy	½ pint of milk
6 ounces white breadcrumbs	1 bay leaf
1 egg yolk	salt and black pepper
	1 gill of double cream
	1 glass of dry sherry

Preparation

Chop the onions finely. Pound the anchovies. Wipe and slice the mushrooms. Preheat the oven to number 5-400 degrees.

Method

Stuffing — Melt the butter in a pan and add the onions, cooking till lightly brown. Now stir in the herbs, breadcrumbs and anchovies. Remove from the heat, cool slightly and blend in the egg yolk until everything is well bound together.

To make the paupiettes — Lay the escalopes flat on the table and place a dollop of stuffing on each. Complete by wrapping the veal round the stuffing and secure all with a wooden cocktail stick.

The sauce — Heat the butter in a large pan and place the paupiettes briefly in it for just long enough to seal the meat and turn it golden brown. Lift them out and transfer them to a deep casserole. Set aside.

Stir into the hot butter the chopped onion and mushrooms and cook for a minute or two before stirring in the flour. Allow to cook gently for three or four minutes before pouring in the milk and bringing quickly to the boil, stirring vigorously.

You should now have a good thick sauce, into which you pour the double cream and sherry. Blend well and season to taste. Pour over the waiting paupiettes with the bay leaf and cover the casserole. Cook in a moderately hot oven (number 5-400 degrees) for 20 minutes.

FRIED VEAL CHINESE STYLE

Scallopines of veal served with bean sprouts, bamboo shoots and water chestnuts on a bed of rice.

To serve 4

THE VEAL

12 x 2 ounces scallopines of veal	8 cups of water
seasoned flour	salt
4 cups of rice	

THE BATTER

8 ounces flour	salt and white pepper
2 eggs	a pinch of sugar
½ pint of milk	a clove of garlic
½ ounce yeast	

THE CHINESE VEGETABLES

4 ounce tin of bean sprouts	a glass of sherry
4 ounce tin of bamboo shoots	soy sauce
4 ounce tin of water chestnuts	1 green pepper
3 ounces flaked almonds	1 onion
4 ounces mushrooms	salt
a clove of garlic	

Preparation

Crush all the garlic. Drain and slice the bamboo shoots, water chestnuts, green pepper, onion and mushrooms. Warm the milk. Boil the rice. Pass the scallopines through the seasoned flour.

Method

Firstly — make the batter by adding the yeast to the warmed milk with the sugar, garlic and seasoning. Allow to stand in a warm place until the mixture begins to bubble. Place the flour in a mixing bowl leaving a well in the centre into which the eggs are broken. Now start whisking the eggs into the flour slowly adding as you do so the warm yeasty milk until you achieve a smooth batter. Set aside to stand.

Next the vegetables. These should all be tipped into a covered pan with the almonds, sherry and soy sauce. Add salt to taste and allow to cook on a low flame for 20 minutes. Meanwhile take the scallopines, dip them into the batter and deep fry until they are crisp and golden.

Assembly

Arrange the scallopines on the bed of rice and surround with the vegetables.

VEAL CORDON BLEU

Veal, ham, emmenthal cheese fried in a crispy coating of breadcrumbs.

To serve 4

4 x 3 ounces escalopes of veal
4 x 3 ounces slices of cooked ham
4 large slices of emmenthal cheese
flour
1 cup of milk
2 eggs
breadcrumbs
black pepper
butter

Preparation
Beat the eggs and milk together to make the egg wash.

Method
Lay the escalopes on the table and place a slice of cheese over each —
season with black pepper and cover with a slice of ham. Press down firmly.
Dust well with flour on both sides, and immerse in the egg wash before
dipping in the breadcrumbs to form an even coating.

Now take a large shallow pan and melt the butter. Fry the veal on both
sides till golden, crisp and just beginning to ooze cheese. Serve at once.

OSSO BUCCO

Knuckles of veal cooked in a rich vegetable and wine sauce.

To serve 6

6 thick slices of shin of veal*	4 tablespoons tomato puree
a little seasoned flour	12 tomatoes
4 cloves of garlic	6 anchovy fillets
4 tablespoons of oil	Parsley
1 spanish onion	salt and black pepper
2 carrots	3 cups of rice
2 sticks of celery	6 cups of water
2 green peppers	2 strands of saffron
1 pint dry white wine	juice of a lemon

Preparation

Pass the veal through the seasoned flour. Crush the garlic. Chop all vegetables very finely except the tomatoes. Peel, seed and chop tomatoes. Pound the anchovy fillets. Chop the parsley. Cook the rice with the saffron. Preheat the oven to number 3-350 degrees.

Method

Take the floured veal and fry on all sides in the hot oil until the meat is sealed and golden brown. Transfer the meat to a deep casserole and set aside.

Using the oil from the veal, throw into the pan the carrotts, green peppers, onions, celery, tomatoes, anchovies, garlic and seasoning. Cook for a few minutes before blending in the tomato puree, wine and lemon juice. Finally tip the vegetable sauce over the knuckles of veal, cover the casserole and bake the whole thing in a slow oven (number 3-350 degrees) for two hours. Adjust the seasoning and sprinkle liberally with chopped parsley before serving on a bed of the rice.

Hints. *Ask the butcher to cut these for you, making sure that he gives you as much meat as bone.

ROOT VEGETABLES

Mr. Lincoln's favourite potatoes

Peel the potatoes and then make a series of cuts through half each potato as if finely slicing but leaving it joined at the base.

Place in a roasting tray, cut side upwards. Half fill the tray with a good seasoned chicken or veal stock and brush the tops with butter. Bake in a moderately hot oven (number 5-400 degrees) until the potatoes have absorbed the stock and are nicely browned. The end result looks very attractive.

Mr. Dowding's favourite potatoes

Peel the potatoes and boil in salted water until almost cooked. Meanwhile fry in plenty of butter, some sliced onion and streaky bacon. Drain the potatoes well, lay in a roasting tray and pile the onions, bacon and butter over them. Place in a very hot oven (number 8-475 degrees) for ten to fifteen minutes.

Boulangere Potatoes

Peel and slice the potatoes thinly. Cut some onion into rings. Take a deep casserole and place in it alternate layers of onion and potato, seasoning each layer and finishing with potato. Pour in the chicken stock to just below the surface, leaving the top layer dry. Brush this well with melted butter, cover and bake in a moderately hot oven (number 5-400 degrees) until cooked. Remove the lid, increase the heat to number 8-475 degrees and brown the top of the potatoes for a further fifteen minutes.

Braised Beetroots

Peel and quarter baby beetroots. Place in a deep casserole and cover well with the chicken stock. Dollop a few knobs of butter on the top. Season with salt and pepper. Cover and cook slowly in a moderate oven (number 4-375 degrees) until the beetroots are tender. Serve with a little liquor and sour cream.

Baked Parsnips and Onions

Peel equal quantities of small onions and baby parsnips and blanch in boiling salted water for five minutes. Drain. Melt some good dripping into a roasting tray and tip the drained vegetables into it. Baste well. Sprinkle with salt and black pepper and bake in a moderately hot oven (number 5-400 degrees) until all are crisp and golden.

GREEN VEGETABLES

Cabbage with Ham, Nuts and Butter
Cook the cabbage in salt water until it is soft but not mushy. Drain.
Meanwhile chop the ham and nuts finely and combine with melted butter.
Place the cabbage in a serving dish and sprinkle the ham, nuts and butter
on the top. Serve immediately.

Cauliflower Polonaise
Boil the cauliflower in salted water, drain and gently divide into flowerets.
Arrange in a serving dish and sprinkle alternate layers of chopped hard
boiled egg, chopped parsley and browned breadcrumbs. Pour over a little
melted butter and place in a hot oven (number 7-450 degrees) for a few
minutes before serving.

Celery Provencale
Fry together onions and garlic in a little oil and when nicely brown throw
in the celery, chopped. Fry gently for a moment before adding some dry
white wine and tinned tomatoes with their juice. Season well. Cover and
simmer very slowly until the celery is tender. Add a little tomato puree and
cook for a further five minutes.

Spinach with Butter and Herbs
Cook the spinach in a small amount of salted water. Drain and squeeze well
to remove all moisture. Chop through roughly. Keep warm. Into a large
frying pan melt an ample knob of butter and sprinkle in a pinch of oregano,
thyme and basil. Add the chopped spinach to the pan and toss well with the
butter and herbs. Serve sizzling hot.

Petit Pois a la Francais
Cook the peas and drain them, reserving enough of the liquor for the
sauce. In this liquor cook some button onions and shredded lettuce, until
the onions are soft. Now, in a separate bowl, beat together an equal
quantity of soft butter and flour (one ounce of each thickens ½ pint of
liquor). Spoon in this thickening and whisk with the liquor until a smooth
sauce has been achieved. Now stir in the peas and serve immediately.

ATHOL BROSE

For those who love a drop of the hard stuff in their pud.

To serve 6

1 pint of double cream
4 tablespoons of thin clear honey
1 large tot of whisky

Method
The great beauty of this sweet is its simplicity. Just whisk all the ingredients together until you have achieved a thick creamy consistency.

Serve into 6 champagne glasses.

BLACK CHERRY FRANGIPANE

An open flan filled with black cherries, almond sponge and topped with icing.

To serve 8

8 ounces shortcrust pastry
1 pound sweet dark pitted cherries

Sponge
6 ounces butter
6 ounces sugar
3 eggs
4 ounces self-raising flour
2 ounces ground almonds
a few drops of almond essence

Icing
8 ounces icing sugar
lemon juice
water

Preparation
Preheat oven to number 4-375 degrees. Line an 8 inch flan tin with the pastry and prick all over with a fork.

Method
Firstly cover the bottom of the flan with the black cherries. Now make the almond sponge by firstly beating together the butter and sugar till almost white. Then add the 3 eggs one by one alternately with three tablespoons of the flour. Fold in the rest of the flour, the almonds and almond essence and spread this mixture over the cherries. Bake in a moderate oven (number 4-375 degrees) for 35 to 40 minutes. Remove and allow to cool.

Make up the icing with the lemon juice and water and spread over the top of the Frangipane.

BROWN BREAD ICE CREAM

An echo from the past and frequently resurrected at The Hungry Monk. Crumbs of brown bread coated in toffee and mixed into ice cream with rum.

To serve 16

½ gallon of vanilla ice cream
5 cups of brown breadcrumbs
4 ounces demerara sugar
4 tots of rum
½ cup of water

Preparation
Take the ice cream out of the deep freeze and allow to slightly thaw.

Method
Firstly, it is necessary to caramelise the brown breadcrumbs by boiling the sugar and water together bringing them to a syrup. Continue to heat until the syrup is fully caramelised (380 degrees to 390 degrees). Stir in the breadcrumbs. Next pour the rum into the ice cream quickly followed by the caramelised breadcrumbs. Blend very swiftly before the breadcrumbs have a chance to form any large lumps.

Pour in the brown bread ice cream into the original container and replace in the freezer.

CHOCOLATE BRANDY CREAM

The most deliciously sickly chocolate mousse of them all – and the most popular pudding at The Hungry Monk from the day it was introduced.

To serve 8

1 pound of best quality plain chocolate – NOT cooking chocolate
½ cup of freshly brewed coffee
1 large tot of brandy
3 eggs
1 disposable hyperdermic syringe which costs about 5p from any chemist

Preparation
Break the chocolate into the top of a double saucepan. Separate the eggs. Whisk egg whites until stiff.

Method
Melt the chocolate together with the coffee into a smooth, thick sauce. Remove the pan from the heat and beat in the egg yolks. Blend thoroughly before finally folding in the beaten egg whites.
Pour the mixture into eight small ramekins and place in the refrigerator. After ¼ hour draw the brandy into the syringe and inject into the centre of each Chocolate Brandy Cream. Return to the refrigerator and allow a further two hours to set.

Variations
Many people prefer chocolate and orange brandy cream as the fresh orange tempers the richness. To make this use only a quarter of a cupful of brewed coffee with the juice and zest ot two oranges.
The other good alternative is to use fruit and nut chocolate.

DANISH CHOCOLATE GATEAU

This gateau almost defies description. It is not really a gateau at all but more a large piece of solid soft chocolate, laden with chunks of wheatmeal biscuit, glace cherries and nuts.

To serve 8—10 (depending on greed)

1 pound of best quality plain chocolate — NOT cooking chocolate
½ cup of freshly brewed coffee
a large tot of rum
6 ounces glace cherries
6 ounces of walnuts, hazelnuts and almonds — mixed
6 ounces wheatmeal biscuits
1 ounce of butter
1 x 6 inch deep cake tin with a false bottom

Preparation
Break the chocolate into the top of a double saucepan. Roughly break the biscuits.

Method
Melt the chocolate together with the coffee and butter into a smooth, thick sauce. Remove from the heat and pour in the rum.

Meanwhile in a separate bowl mix together the broken biscuits, nuts and glace cherries, before pouring over the molten chocolate. Stir thoroughly until everything is evenly coated with chocolate. Now transfer into the cake tin, smooth over the top and place in the refrigerator. Allow 12 hours to set.

Variations
Lovers of bananas might like to ring the changes by replacing the glace cherries with chopped bananas. In this case take care to completely cover with chocolate any banana that might be protruding from the top of the gateau to stop it going brown.

BUTTERSCOTCH FUDGE GATEAU

A variation on the theme of Danish Chocolate Gateau where the chocolate is replaced with butterscotch.

To serve 8—10

6 ounces butter
6 ounces golden syrup
8 ounces stoned dates
4 ounces glace cherries
4 ounces mixed nuts — hazelnuts, almonds, walnuts
8 ounces wheatmeal biscuits
1 x 6 inch deep cake tin with a false bottom

Preparation
Crush half the biscuits and crumble the other half.

Method
Combine the butter and golden syrup in a heavy pan. As soon as the butter has melted, bring to the boil, whisking all the time. Boil for no longer than two to three minutes still whisking. Set aside. Take a large bowl and mix together all the other ingredients — dates, cherries, nuts and all the biscuits. Now pour the butterscotch sauce over this mixture and make sure everything is evenly coated with the sauce. Transfer the mixture into the cake tin. Smooth over the top and place in the refrigerator — allow 12 hours to set. 🍀

Hints. Do not over boil the butter and golden syrup otherwise it will become brittle and hard to eat.

*Lord, I am a worm
and no man*

*Filled with all
manner of weakness*

*Wretched, unspeakable
a thing of straw*

Sinful, guilty

*Most abject of
all mankind*

*In fact, it puzzles
me rather*

*That considering all
these disadvantages . . .*

*I'm such a
splendid cook!*

BUTTERSCOTCH PANCAKES

Pancakes soaked in a rich butterscotch sauce and baked in the oven.

To serve 6

12 pancakes — see page 28
6 ounces butter
6 ounces golden syrup

Method
Firstly fold each pancake twice to form a triangle and arrange them in the bottom of a shallow fireproof dish.
Next make a butterscotch sauce by boiling together melted butter and golden syrup taking care to whisk continuously from the moment when the butter melts until you have boiled for two to three minutes. Remove from the heat and pour over the waiting pancakes. Warm thoroughly in a low oven.

CHOCOLATE and ORANGE CHEESECAKE

An orange flavoured cheesecake on a base of plain chocolate in a crunchy wheatmeal case.

To serve 8

4 ounces wheatmeal biscuits
1 ounce butter
¼ pound plain Bournville chocolate
water
1½ pound cream cheese
3 fluid ounces of concentrated Bird's Eye Florida orange juice
2 ounces castor sugar

Preparation
Crumble the biscuits. Melt the chocolate with a little water.

Method
Melt the butter and stir in the crumbled biscuits. Now line an eight inch flan tin with an even layer of the biscuit mixture and pour over the bottom a coating of melted chocolate an eighth of an inch thick. Do not attempt to spread the chocolate as it will disturb the biscuit base. Place in the refrigerator.

While all this is setting hard beat the cream cheese, sugar and the orange concentrate into a smooth consistency ready to be spread over the hardened chocolate. When this has been done, replace the whole thing in the refrigerator and chill thoroughly.

COLD SOUFFLE
GRAND MARNIER

or how to share two tots of Grand Marnier between eight people.

To serve 6—8

6 eggs
½ pint double cream
6 ounces castor sugar
2 large tots of Grand Marnier
½ ounce leaf gelatine
¼ pint of water

Preparation
Whip the cream until stiff. Separate the eggs and beat the whites until stiff.
Soften the gelatine in the ¼ pint of cold water. Put a double saucepan on
to boil.

Method
Tip the egg yolks, sugar and Grand Marnier into the top of the double
saucepan and whisk continually until thick. Take off the heat and set aside.
Now heat the softened gelatine in the ¼ pint of water and stir it into the
egg yolk mixture. The next move is to transfer this to a bowl and leave it
in the refrigerator until it begins to set. Once this has happened remove
from the refrigerator and gently fold in first the whisked egg whites and then
the cream.

Transfer the mixture into a souffle dish and allow to set in the refrigerator.

MERINGUES FILLED
with APPLE CHEESE

As good as it sounds

To serve 8

THE MERINGUES	THE FILLING

THE MERINGUES
5 egg whites
8 ounces castor sugar
2 ounces icing sugar

THE FILLING
4 large cooking apples
a knob of butter
1 ounce demerara sugar
1 pound cream cheese

Preparation
Sieve the castor sugar and icing together. Grease a baking tray, lightly but thoroughly. Preheat the oven to number 1-290 degrees.

Method
Whisk the egg whites stiffly so that the points will stand upright on the whisk. Then add a quarter of the sugar and whisk stiffly again. Now gently fold in the rest of the sugar and transfer the mixture into a piping bag with a plain nozzel. Dispense eight good large meringues onto the baking tray and bake in a very cool oven (number 1-290 degrees with the door open) until the meringues are crisp but not dried up.

Next the apple cheese filling
Peel, core and slice the apples and gently cook them with the brown sugar and butter until they are soft and mushy. Remove from the heat and beat in the cream cheese until you have a smooth cream. Transfer to a bowl and chill.

Assembly
Shortly before serving, slice the top off each meringue and spoon in a generous portion of the apple cheese allowing it to over flow down the sides of the meringue before replacing the top.

Hints. Many people prefer to use rice paper to eradicate any possibility of the meringues sticking to the baking tray.

Variations
These are practically limitless but we think the best are meringues with lemon cheese, apple and raisin cheese, fresh strawberry cheese and damson cheese.

MARRON SYLLABUB

A delicious blend of marrons and whipped cream.

To serve 12

1 pound 12 ounces marrons (whole tinned unsweetened)
1 pint double cream
2 large tots of brandy
4 ounces dark brown sugar

Preparation
Take half the marrons and pound to a puree, chop the other half roughly and combine with the puree and a little juice from the tin.

Method
Whisk the cream until stiff. In a separate bowl blend the marron mixture, the brandy and the sugar. Now gently fold the cream into the marrons and transfer into twelve champagne glasses. Allow to stand in the refrigerator for two to three hours.

DRY MEASURES · (Ounces to Grams)

IMPERIAL AND AMERICAN Ounces	METRIC Grams
1	28
1¾	50
2	56
3	85
3½	100
4	113
5	143
16 (1 lb)	453
2 lb. 3¼ oz.	1000 (1 kilogram)

LIQUID MEASURES · (Litres to Pints)
(Table A)

METRIC		IMPERIAL	
Litres	Millilitres	Fluid Ounces	Pints
		(nearest equivalent)	(nearest equivalent)
1	1000	35¼	1¾
¾	750	26½	1¼
*	568	20	1
½	500	17½	¾
¼	250	8¾	½
½	'25	4½	¼

LIQUID MEASURES · (International Equivalents)
(Table B)

IMPERIAL	AMERICAN (US)	METRIC (nearest equivalent)
1 teaspoon**	1¼	6 millilitres
1 tablespoon or 2 dessertspoons**	1¼	19 millilitres
3½ fl. oz.	6⅔ tablesoons	100 millilitres
4 fl. oz.	½ cup (¼ pint US)	⅛ litre
¼ pint or 1 gill	5 fl. oz.	150 millilitres
8 fl. oz.	1 cup (½ pint US)	¼ litre
½ pint of 1 cup**	10 fl. oz.	300 millilitres
16 fl. oz.	1 pint (16 fl. oz. US)	*
1 pint (20 fl. oz.)	20 fl. oz.	600 millilitres
32 fl. oz.	1 quart (2 pints US)	*
34 fl. oz.	4⅓ cups	1 litre
1 quart (2 pints)	40 fl. oz.	1.2 litres

** British Standard Measures

* Footnote for Liquid Measures: It can be seen from these tables that 1 PINT is not a workable fraction of A LITRE; whereas all the other fractions given equate to each other in a reasonably practical way.

For example: 1 fluid ounce = 28.4 millilitres.
It is therefore more practical to take *30 millilitres* as the metric equivalent.

OVEN TEMPERATURE CONVERSIONS

Celsius or Centigrade °C	Fahrenheit °F	Gas Mark	
110	225	¼	very cool
130	250	½	very cool
140	275	1	cool
150	300	2	cool
170	325	3	moderate
180	350	4	moderate
190	375	5	moderately hot
200	400	6	moderately hot
220	425	7	hot
230	450	8	very hot
240	475	9	very hot